RHYMES WITH REASON

RHYMES WITH REASON

Neville Peace

ARTHUR H. STOCKWELL LTD
Torrs Park, Ilfracombe, Devon, EX34 8BA
Established 1898
www.ahstockwell.co.uk

British Library Cataloguing-in-Publication Data.
A catalogue record for this book is available
from the British Library.

ISBN 978-0-7223-4604-4
Printed in Great Britain by
Arthur H. Stockwell Ltd
Torrs Park   Ilfracombe
Devon EX34 8BA

CONTENTS

SHRINKAGE

When I was a small boy I thought,
When I'm older I'll be closer to heaven,
But eventually shrinkage has set in
And I'm now only five foot seven.
Once I was taller and at five foot ten
I was as close as I would get, ah well!
Instead of being closer to heaven,
I'm now much nearer to hell.

I feel like a woollen jumper
That's been put in water too hot,
Instead of fitting an adult,
It would now just fit a young tot.
If I continue shrinking at this rate,
I won't become just small,
I will eventually disappear
And become nothing at all!

THE LETTER

I'm writing you this little note,
I can't use the phone, I have a sore throat,
To send you my latest news
Together with a few of my views.
Oh! I do like a good moan.

My back is full of twinges,
And both my knees require new hinges.
And what about the price of meat?
Please don't mention my poor old feet.
Oh! I do like a good moan.

The weather is appalling,
The neighbour's kids are bawling.
I have to cut the lawn, but the grass is wet,
And this is not as bad as it can get.
Oh! I do like a good moan.

My elbows are creaking,
And my water tank's leaking.
I need to see the doctor, but can't get a date,
So I called 999, but the ambulance was late.
Oh! I do like a good moan.

Newspapers are all depressing,
MPs are fiddling and messing,
Our footballers are paid too much,
And our cricketers don't win much.
Oh! I do like a good moan.

My telly's on the blink,
And I don't know what to think.
Cold-callers are a pain,
They cause an ache in my brain.
Oh! I do like a good moan.

Now I've had a good moan I feel much better,
So I don't think I'll bother to send you this letter.

WHAT A QUESTION

When I misbehaved my mum would say,
"Do you want a good hiding?"
What sort of question is that, pray?
And what part was good I had difficulty in finding.

It was a rhetorical question, I dare answer not,
A yes or no and the result would have been the same.
I would have had a hiding good or not,
So I kept my head down and played the game.

I didn't always escape her wrath,
And she had a mean right arm.
I learned to work the odds out, I was reasonable at math –
But, whenever I had deserved a tanning, it did me no harm.

CANCER

"It's malignant," said the doctor, "I'm sorry but it's true."
"Oh dear," I remarked, "I'd rather have the flu!
So what do we do, what's the treatment?" I said.
"We'll give some radiation that will turn you bright red,
Then when that's over, some chemo, no doubt,
You'll be violently sick, and your hair will fall out!"

So I had all the treatment, it lasted a while,
Sometimes I cried, but occasionally I'd smile.
It was true what he'd told me, I didn't feel well,
But it was doing me good, so thought, 'What the hell.'
Now it's all over, and I'm full of good health,
It's the doctor needs convincing, I'm quite sure myself!

A SONNET TO MY WIFE

You are the fresh brightening dawn each day I seek,
The snow-covered Highland mountain peak,
The heather-clad valleys where deer leap.

You are my sunshine in a bright blue sky,
A moonlit night in mid July,
The open common where skylarks fly.

You are the restless waves on a sandy shore,
The rippling streams across the moor,
The golden corn that's ready to store.

You are the birds in song, the buzzing bees,
The woodland glade and sun-dappled trees,
The rolling hills and tree-covered valleys.

You are my comfort at each day's end,
My wife, my love and my best friend.

THINGS EVERY PARENT SHOULD KNOW

Where does all the water go when the tide goes out?
Why do I have a nose when a pig has got a snout?
Why are mountaintops cold when they're closer to the sun?
Why can horses trot and gallop when I can only run?
Where do sneezes come from and why do I get stitch?
When I had the measles what was it made them itch?
How does a big oak tree from an acorn grow?
What makes all the streams and the rivers flow?
Where do clouds come from and where do they go to?
What holds the sun in place and why is the sky blue?
Why is snow white and why does Granddad snore?
And could I have a magic carpet on my bedroom floor?
Why do pigs grunt, lambs bleat and cows moo
When dogs bark, cats meow and pigeons coo?
What holds a bubble together and can you touch the sky?
Where do stars go at daytime and how do you get them in your eye?
Why are cricket pitches green when pitch is really black?
And when I'm learning new skills where do I find the knack?
Where do babies come from and can we have another?
I'd like one to play with, a little baby brother.

DEMENTIA

Dementia is not a dirty word,
Just an illness of which you've heard.
It's not infectious or contagious,
Views like that are quite outrageous.

This came to us without a choice,
We didn't pick, we had no voice.
So when you see us, be thankful do,
It's we who have it, it could be you.

A SMALL BOY'S CHRISTMAS

At last it's Christmas morning, let's see what Santa's brought,
A Rupert book, lead soldiers and a lovely wooden fort,
Roller skates, some marbles and a model car to make,
A bagatelle board and . . . Mark, Mark, it's time to wake.

Oh no, that's Mother calling, those toys were all a dream.
Now that I am really awake, let's see if Santa's been.
Ah, there's the Christmas stocking hanging on a hook,
There's an orange and an apple and a comic book,
A tram conductor's cap and badge and a bag of sweets,
A lump of coal to light the fire, giving Yuletide heat.
Some shiny, Brassoed pennies and a snakes and ladders game,
But that's OK, because the boy next door had much the same.
Our dads had gone to fight a war, mums did the best they could,
And though we were quite young, I think we understood.
And only just last week Dad sent our mum a letter,
It said the war will soon be over and next year will be better.

GLENYS

Oh yes, I've had a life, I did my thing and the memories are still there,
Because I can't recall them all, doesn't mean the cupboard is bare.
With just a little prompting and a photograph or two,
I can remember things that once to me were new.
The fresh-tilled earth, the waving wheat, the smell of new-mown hay,
A clear blue sky, the buzzing bees on a sunny, summer day.
The flowers in spring, the birds that sing, are still a thrill to me,
I can sing, dance and smile, and laugh out loud with glee.
Everyone is important including you and me,
We all have gifts to share and the best thing is they're free.
I deal with what life brings me, what will be will be,
And when tomorrow morning comes, I will still be me.

ANOTHER VIEW

"I'm giving Christmas a miss this year," said the turkey to her mate.
"I saw what they did to cousin Tom, and it's left me in a state.
They put him in a freezer, and what gives me the shivers,
Before they put him in the cold they plucked out all his feathers.

"It's hard to have a happy Christmas when you're naked and you're cold,
And after all is said and done, he wasn't very old.
As Christmas Day approached, from the freezer they took him out,
Amid the smell of Christmas pudding and a pan of boiling sprouts.

"And then, to compound the earlier slaughter,
Where they put the sage and onion, fair made my two eyes water.
So yes, I'm giving Christmas a miss this year, it really is the dregs,
I'm going to keep my head well down and continue laying eggs."

THE BOX

When you are born you have a box
In which you keep life's treasures –
Your mother's smile, your father's laugh
And other childhood pleasures.
The grandparents who, when crossing busy roads,
Always held your hand.
The patient teacher who took time to explain
When you didn't understand.
Those holidays by the sea, all the pets you had
And also your first bike.
The clubs you joined, all the friends you made
And the bank holiday hike.
The day your girlfriend dumped you,
The week your pet dog died.
All memories and events, both sad and happy,
Are tucked away inside.
Your first day at work,
And the office girls you couldn't pull,
All these things go in the box
And yet it's never full.
Then one day your grandma dies,
And the box seems suddenly empty,
But that memory now is in a new format,
And still of life there's plenty.
If you're lucky you get married
And have children of your own,
They have boxes of their own to fill,
And so your life goes on.
In your box you note their first faltering steps
And the first words that they utter,
Until the teenage years come along
And it all becomes grunt and mutter.
You keep adding to the box
With every deed they did,
But the box never becomes quite full
Until you close the lid.

FANCY THAT

"What's for afters?" I hear you cry.
"Is it lemon meringue or apple pie?"
For pudding I like sticky toffee,
Or something tasty made with coffee.
Black Forest gateau is a huge temptation,
Whilst peach Melba was a great sensation.
With fresh fruit salad, sherry trifle, tortes as cold as ice,
Crème brûlée and crêpes Suzette, we're all spoilt for choice.
But whatever sweets you think about, of what desserts you dream,
There surely is no finer treat than English strawberries and cream.

EVERY DAY'S A GOOD DAY

The green sword tips that pierce the snow
Foretell a bright, golden glow.
As daffodils and narcissi grow,
To brighten the view when March winds blow.

High mountain peaks are shrouded in mists,
While bright-green meadows are sunbeam-kissed.
Lazy flowing rivers meandering to the sea
Meet the crashing waves that spray you and me.

Russet-carpeted paths through woods do wander,
While busy squirrels hide nuts here and yonder.
The crunch of leaves warn the shy deer,
Who conceal themselves as we get near.

Then comes winter's icy blow,
With rain and sleet and freezing snow.
The Christmas magic and twinkling lights,
Children's eyes aglow on this night of nights.

Every day's a good day, the sun is in the sky,
If obscured by cloud right now, it will be there by and by.

NO PROBLEMS

I no longer run up stairs, but walk them slowly one by one.
There is no need to rush and dash, just quietly get things done.
There was a time when my hair was so much thicker,
But now I can wash and dry it very much quicker.
The veggie patch I could once turn over in a day,
But now it takes three days to dig, there is no other way.
When I stoop to pick things up, I bend my back and not my knee,
I wonder who that old man is, then I realise it's me!

AN UDDER TALE

My husband is a thespian in the local am-dram group,
Twice a year they produce a show, they're a lively little troupe.
This year he's in a panto, but he doesn't have to talk,
The panto they are putting on is *Jack and the Beanstalk*.

He doesn't have a major part, but one vital to the plot.
He isn't Baron Hardup and the dame he's certainly not.
He isn't Idle Jack and for the giant he's much too small,
During the auditions he almost didn't gain a role at all.

I'm sure you've guessed which part he plays by now,
Yes you're right, I'm married to the back half of a cow.

TOGETHERNESS

We've had some laughs, we've shed some tears,
We've had adventures despite our fears.

We've had our ups, we've had our downs,
We've had our smiles, we've had some frowns.

We've had some luck, some good, some bad,
We've been mostly happy, occasionally sad.

Through all the stress together we've coped,
When things were grim, for better times we hoped.

We've worked together and for each other,
Neither needing nor wanting another lover.

Generally life's been good for us,
So we face the future without any fuss.

SHEBA

My pal had a dog and Sheba was her name,
Paws, ears and nose was her favourite game.
Her eyes were brown and shiny bright,
Her lustrous coat as black as night.

Now she romps in celestial fields,
Her bark is heard no more.
But, in dreams, her master still takes
Her gently proffered paw.

And when, at last, he crosses that great divide,
What greetings there will be,
And together they will walk those meadows
For all eternity.

LIMERICKS

There was a young man from Stroud,
Whose laugh was exceedingly loud.
As people took cover,
They said to each other,
"He certainly stands out in a crowd."

A haughty young man from Cam,
With disdain said, "Do you know who I am?"
Several people muttered,
One or two stuttered,
But most folk said, "We don't give a damn."

A young lady from the WI,
Thought her culinary skills were quite high,
But as a matter of fact,
And to be quite exact,
Her ideas were just pie in the sky.

There was a young man from Redditch,
Who, whenever he ran caught the stitch.
To alleviate the pain,
He decided to train,
And now he can race with no hitch.

There was a young man from Lydney,
Who loved pies, steak and kidney.
He ate such a pile,
He can't walk a mile,
So they call him Stationary Sidney.

There was a young lady from Brum,
In the winter her hands would go numb.
She said, "I would love,
A warm pair of gloves,
Then in the snow I could have lots more fun."

WHAT A NIGHT

It's Christmas Eve and Santa's busiest night,
The presents are all loaded and the sleigh is ready for flight.
The workshops have been cleaned and now look quite pristine;
His nine reindeer have been groomed and to go are very keen.

His first deliveries go smoothly and on time,
At each stop he finds a glass of sherry, that he thinks is fine.
Presents are delivered and he drinks the Bristol Cream,
And progress along the route goes just like a dream.

Santa is quite partial to a sherry or two,
And during the night he drinks quite a few!
He gradually exceeds his quota and becomes very merry,
His nose, like Rudolph's, shines out like a berry.

His eyes are shining brightly and his cheeks have a ruddy glow,
He emerges from the chimney and groans, "It's beginning to snow!"
Now his satnav isn't working, and his maps he's left behind,
But he still has presents to deliver and chimney pots to find.

He presses on through the night,
Delivering presents left and right.
He delivers presents, but not where they're intended,
But still has time to keep those sherry glasses upended.

Now his eyes are bloodshot and both his temples throbbing,
All that he can see are eighteen reindeer tails a-bobbing!
The address labels on the parcels are no longer clear,
And the presents are delivered to the wrong recipients, I fear.

At last the sacks are empty, the presents have all gone,
The dawn is just breaking with the emerging sun.
Santa now is very confused, the herd of reindeer in disarray.
He said, "Thank goodness that's over; tonight's been quite a day!"

The moral of this story is,
If you want the presents you ask for, be early on the list,
Before dear old Santa gets totally Brahms and Liszt.

WEDDING DAY WISHES

May you always be as happy as you are today,
May good luck and fortune come your way.
May your troubles be few and far between,
May you always be strong and follow your dreams.
May your life together be faithful and true,
May you both be successful in all that you do.

THE THIN GREEN LINE

The dotted green line crosses the ridge and descends into the hollow,
On the OS maps, with your fingertips, it is so very easy to follow,
But in the fields of grass, green's not easily seen –
So why, instead, don't they paint it red;
Then rambling would be quite serene.

Dedicated to all those ramblers who, like me, have occasionally found themselves on the ground in a different place to where they thought they were on the map.

A WOMAN'S TOUCH

The time of year has come to decorate the tree.
Father says, "Lights are technical and so are down to me."
From the loft he retrieves the Christmas tree delights –
Baubles, candles, glitter and the box of Christmas lights.

"When I packed the lights away they were working fine,
But before I put them on the tree I'll check them one more time."
He plugs them in and switches on,
But of a light there isn't one.

He mutters quietly under his breath, his blood pressure heightened.
He then proceeds to check that each bulb in its holder is tightened.
Once more he switches on, but still there is no glimmer;
His jaw now tightens another notch, his face is looking grimmer.

Now the bulbs in series are connected and so there is no doubt,
Like trade unions on strike, it's one out all out.
He now patiently replaces each bulb in turn with a spare,
And at each replacement switches on with a prayer.

After trying a spare in every holder, there's still no sign of light,
He now is very angry, his jaw muscles extremely tight.
He says, "There must be more than one bulb blown,
I'll have to test each with a multimeter," he mutters with a groan.

After testing each one and finding them all good,
The problem he now thinks is quite understood.
The fault is a broken wire and he'll never find that,
A new set must be purchased, so he gets his coat and hat.

At the store he is greeted with a bewildering array
Of lights in chains round trees on display.
Some just switch on, some go on and off, some chase along,
Some with selectable sequences, and some even with a song.

Eventually he makes his selection and returns home.
When he arrives there his face just turns to stone.
The tree is all decorated and the lights all aglow,
The new set he has purchased, he now is ready to throw.

Through gritted teeth he says,
"Very clever, which electrician did you use?"
His wife just smiles sweetly and says,
"I simply changed the fuse!"

SPORTING FRIENDS

We ran our races and did our best,
Enjoyed the freedom of shorts and vest.
The spirit to run, it is still there,
But it's now much harder to vacate the chair.
The successes enjoyed were all too few,
But with every one our confidence grew.
For all of us each prize meant more
Than cabinets full of trophies galore.
But more precious than that are, still today,
The friends we made along the way.

SPORTING HEROES

My hero is the teenage Olympic finalist who lines up full of hope,
But is sadly beaten by a cheat, who is full of dope.
One day, with training, the young athlete will be a winner,
But the cheat will always be a sinner.
The youngster will know his achievements are his own,
But the cheat's successes will be due to chemicals alone.

FOR CARERS

Don't waste time with anger,
Count slowly from one to ten,
Or walk away for a little while,
And then come back again.

You've faced challenges all your life,
And they've all been overcome.
The challenge you face right now
Is just another one.

So sleep easy in your bed at night,
Knowing you've done your best.
Have as much rest as you can,
For tomorrow's another test.

And when things do go wrong,
Something spilt on your brand-new rug,
Don't waste time with anger,
Just have a little hug.

A NIGHT AT THE RACES

After a pleasant meal in friendly company,
We could have slept like logs,
But instead, our fortunes to make,
We all went to the dogs.

We queued up to put money
On a hound in coloured coat,
But after the race we could
Have grabbed him by the throat.

There were a dozen or so
Giving the bookies pound notes by the score,
But to collect their winnings
There were always less than four.

While the race is on the punters yell and shout,
But the bookies were all calm,
They were well aware that their bags of cash
Will never come to harm.

On the long-standing premise that
It is better to give than to receive,
Feel sorry for bookies with their bags of cash
And crocodile tears (not hearts) on their sleeve.

KAY

1933 was a good year, the year that Kay was born,
And as babies are wont to do, I guess that was early morn.
The world was different then, no worse, no better,
To communicate you just sent a letter.
No e-mail then nor mobile phone,
Home entertainment was radio and gramophone.

Milk, bread and coal by horse and cart were delivered to you,
So you see home deliveries are really nothing new.
No health and safety then to spoil the fun,
And we played happily in the sun.
With consummate ease we climbed up trees,
And what did it matter if we grazed our knees!

Bills were paid in pounds, shillings and pence
And even the farthing was fêted,
But that was long before we all became metricated.
We travelled by train, tram or bus,
And waited our turn without any fuss.
Our tables we learned by heart and we knew,
Right from a gross down to two times two.

Biros had not been invented, we did our lessons with ink and pen,
Row on row of copperplate, and then we did it all again.
We can now send men to the moon and back, put telescopes in space,
But does this technology make the world a better place?
The most important things are your family and your friends,
For they will help you through the difficult times life sends.

All these changes you have lived through,
Facing hardships, but enjoying pleasures too.
Now Sid met Kay on the dance floor, where he swept her off her feet,
Dancing was then strict tempo; rock and roll had not hit the street.
In 1955 they were married, but here's the thing,
While Snow White married a prince, Kay White married a King.

CHRISTMAS PUDDINGS

I'm making Christmas puddings for friends and family,
And while I'm at it I'm making one for me.
I have all the ingredients quite handy,
The dry ones, the wet ones and a bottle of brandy.

So in the mixing bowl go suet, breadcrumbs and flour,
With salt and spices mixed well, but for under an hour.
Then stir in the sugars, and all the dried fruit
Plus chopped almonds, grated apple and carrot.

Then mix together three beaten eggs, two tablespoons of brandy,
With finely grated rind and juice of orange and lemon, just handy.
This latter mix is then stirred into the dry ingredients,
Well mixed together, with another slurp of brandy, that's expedient.

This mixture is then evenly divided
And put into greased basins already provided.
Each basin is covered in greaseproof paper and foil,
Then into the slow cooker for twelve hours to boil.

After cooling them down, they are basted with brandy,
Then wrapped in greaseproof paper and foil, they keep quite handy.
On Christmas Day, I'll reheat a slice, in the microwave of course,
Then all I'll need to do is make a drop of brandy sauce.

OH! THE WEATHER

The rain comes down again
And people start to complain.
The sun then comes out
And, oh dear, we have a drought.
The snow and ice then come to town
And everybody wears a frown.
The further outlook is quite bleak –
I wonder what weather we'll have *next* week.

ALF'S AMBLE

We moved out from St Bees,
With bright sunshine on our knees,
We were determined, come what may,
To walk across England to Robin Hood's Bay.

So with toes dipped in the sea, and a pebble to carry,
We strolled along, but had time to tarry.
Jill, Paul, Carol, Steve, Catherine and Rich were all mates,
And had flown the Atlantic from the United States.

Joy, Vicky and Margaret from down under had come,
Simone, Ken and me completed the sum.
With Dave there to guide us we couldn't go wrong,
And to keep things light-hearted, Jill gave us a song.

Through Sandwith, Moor Row and Cleator we went,
Before the long climb up over Dent.
Descending to Nannycatch, Ken took a tumble,
But was soon on his feet and without any grumble.

Soon after that Ennerdale Bridge was in sight,
Where at the Shepherds Arms we all spent the night.
Then down to Ennerdale Water, a tricky few miles,
Till we crossed over the bridge with quite a few smiles.

On to Black Sail Hut, then a climb up Loft Beck,
So hard to keep going and not become a wreck.
Then on to Honister from where we descended,
But just before Seatoller, Joy was upended.

The game lady got up and carried on without procrastination,
And we all arrived safely at our next destination.
We set off from Rosthwaite next morning at nine,
And strolled up Stonethwaite Beck, the weather still fine.

There followed a steady climb up Greenup Gill,
Then a scramble up Lining Crag, oh, what a hill.
Then along the ridge to Helm Crag, climbed by some without fear,
Then a steep, stony descent into Grasmere.

From Grasmere to Mill Bridge and a steady climb to Grisedale Tarn.
Thence past the 'Parting Stone', down to Glenridding without harm,
To celebrate Carol's birthday in proper style,
With cake and candles and Carol's perfect smile.

Next day we climbed to Boredale Hause, Angle Tarn;
The Knott then Kidsty Pike,
The highest point on our route, it was a hefty hike.
Then down and along Haweswater, then on to Shap,
Today it was Catherine and then Carol who had a mishap.

A quiet, undulating stroll that was fairly even,
Led us from Shap to Kirkby Stephen.
A steady climb to Nine Standards Rigg,
Shrouded in mist (no sun),
Then a meander across the bog,
We would have gladly missed (such fun)!

From Keld another climb to lead-mining ruins
And then across more mire,
Across the Swale River we observed typical farms of Yorkshire.
A drop down cobbled tracks that was mercifully brief,
Then a gentle little stroll into the village of Reeth.

From there to Marrick Priory, then across meadows green,
Up to Whitecliffe Wood and Richmond Castle was very soon seen.
A short stay in Richmond, for Vicky to go shopping, then all hale
We marched down the river to Bolton-on-Swale.

More farmland followed, then roads to Danby Wiske,
Onwards we marched to the A19, to cross an inevitable risk.
Shortly after at Parkhouse we arrived,
With a welcoming drink we were pleasantly surprised.

From Ingleby Cross a roller-coaster day to Clay Bank Top,
Then onwards and upwards to Bloworth Crossing for a short stop.
Followed by a long trudge to The Lion Inn,
Where we were oh, so glad to stumble in.

From Blakey Ridge along road and moor,
To Glaisdale village to rest feet so sore.
Then on to Beggars Bridge for a photo shoot,
And Arncliffe Wood and River Esk to Grosmont, where the trains all hoot.

Now the last day and it starts with a climb,
And our view of the sea, since St Bees, for the first time.
Still more moorland, woods and lanes and we are on our toes,
The closer to the coast we get, the more the excitement grows.

Then our first view of Robin Hood's Bay, a wonderful sight to greet,
Where we cast in all our pebbles and dampen our feet.
So this is where our journey ends
With satisfaction and twelve new friends.

I WAS THERE

I wanted to be sure, but I was indecisive.
I wanted to help, but I was ineffective.
I wanted to be understood, but I was incoherent.
I wanted to be skilful, but I was incompetent.
I wanted to be caring, but I was inconsiderate.
I wanted to be useful, but I was inadequate.
I wanted to be careful, but I was incautious.
I wanted to stand out, but I was inconspicuous.
I wanted to be available, but I was inaccessible.
I wanted to be good, but I was incorrigible.
I wanted to be free, but I was incommunicado.
I wanted to be recognised, but I was incognito.
I wanted to finish, but I was *in perpetuum*.

SNAPSHOTS OF 2014

The jet stream was way off course – again,
And January burst in with wind and rain.
Throughout the month the weather was drear,
For those in floods, not a happy New Year.

Eventually January was spent, 'twas as if it never existed,
But still that pesky, pouring rain persisted.
Most of February was much the same,
So the big debate was who to blame.

While from the west the winds did blow,
Out in Sochi they were making snow.
Then at last the sun came out,
And four months later we were in a drought.

Then, once again, the Crimea became news,
With Ukraine and Russia holding different views.
The Rugby Six Nations by Ireland was won,
Brian O'Driscoll became, briefly, Dublin's favourite son.

In the World Twenty20 series, England played the Netherlands,
It was towards the end of March, and our fate was in our hands.
But, surprise, surprise, surprise, we lost every single wicket!
We thought the Dutch were friends, so that really wasn't cricket.

Little Prince George to the Antipodes did go,
With the Duke and Duchess of Cambridge in tow.
He was a big hit down under, but here's the thing,
Will they still want him there when he is the King?

The euro and local elections came and went,
By the size of the turnout it was a non-event.
Stephen Sutton died, but in his young life he achieved more
Than all those politicians who knock on your door.

We had varied sport all summer long,
World Cup football in Rio, what went wrong?
Once again the English team did their best,
And once again, not good enough against the rest.

In the tests against Sri Lanka, we should win they reckoned.
Sadly we failed, but at least we came second!
Even Wimbledon was a big let-down,
As Andy Murray lost his crown.

We had the Tour de France cycle race
In Yorkshire, where the start took place.
At the Commonwealth Games England topped the medal table,
Just to show that at some sports we are very able.

In Switzerland the European Athletic Championships were held,
And England once again excelled.
Rory McIlroy won the Open and the PGA,
England beat India in the tests, so a big hurray!

Our women won the Rugby World Cup,
And Europe retained the Ryder Cup.
Then summer slowly slipped away,
Replaced by autumn's skies of grey.

Too soon the end of year comes into view,
But before that day I wish a happy Christmas to you.
Soon it will seem that 2014 had never been,
So I wish you all a healthy and happy 2015!

BABIES

A baby is a miracle, but almost helpless when first born,
They can do very little for themselves in their early form.
I always think of their actions as defined by four S's –
They can suckle, smile, sleep and soil their nappies.

They can cry, of course, but that doesn't fit with letter S,
But their crying usually indicates that they are in distress.
Mothers soon recognise the different yells, and their babies pacify,
While fathers struggle by trial and error to stop their babies' cry.

Then they start talking and can say how they feel each day,
But then a complete new can of worms comes into play.
How to explain the meaning of words and when to use I not me –
Thank goodness we have a thesaurus and a dictionary.